# The Tithing Principle

# The
# Tithing
# Principle

## Understanding Why We Give
## Tom Felder

BEACON HILL PRESS
OF KANSAS CITY

Copyright 2011
by Tom Felder and Beacon Hill Press of Kansas City

ISBN 978-0-8341-2597-1

Printed in the
United States of America

Cover Design: J.R. Caines
Inside Design: Sharon Page

**Library of Congress Cataloging-in-Publication Data**
Felder, Tom.
   The tithing principle : understanding why we give / Tom Felder.
       p. cm.
   Includes bibliographical references (p.     ).
   ISBN 978-0-8341-2597-1 (pbk.)
   1. Tithes—Biblical teaching. 2. Christian giving—Biblical teaching. I. Title.
   BS680.T56F45 2010
   248'.6—dc22

                                                    2010044923


10 9 8 7 6 5 4 3 2 1

# Contents

# Foreword

A quick look at society reveals that money, un-like any other physical object, is inseparably tied to human emotion and the perception of power. Anyone who has indulged in an extravagant gift for a loved one, and worried about a utility bill on the same day, knows this well. In *The Tithing Principle*, Tom Felder has captured a character-istic of money that often goes unnoticed: money is spiritual! Our relationship with money and our relationship with the Lord are integrated. Specifi-cally, the concept of tithing has been part of the church since its inception. Tithing is a blessing. It is a Christian principle that is foundational to the faith journey of both the local and global church, and it needs to play a vital role in modern dia-logue of the Christian faith.

Tom Felder and I began talking in 2009 about the lack of resources that address tithing head-on. From that point on, resource development regarding tithing became a primary priority for the entire Stewardship Ministry team. That's why *The Tithing Principle* exists: to provide a story-oriented resource to both pastors and laypeople that makes the concept of faithful tithing real and relatable.

*A culture of faithful tithing encourages the development of church members who are not just involved, but also invested in the ministry and mission of the church: to make Christlike disciples in the nations.*

Thanks to my father and mother, tithing has been an integral part of my spiritual walk since I was very young. When I was in sixth grade, I got my first "real" job driving a Ford 8N tractor to rake hay. I was still too young to lift the hay bales, but at the end of a long day of hard work I was paid ten dollars—an earth-shattering amount to a twelve year old in 1973. Glowing, I brought my earnings home to show my mother. Here it was, proof that I was a full-fledged hardworking man. My mother immediately instructed me to tithe ten percent—a whole dollar! Tithing became real to me in that moment. For an instant, I felt the pang of sacrifice. It was time for a youthful reevaluation of life, priorities, and obedience. Jesus had saved me from my sins, now it was time to make Him Lord of my paycheck. The least I could do to say thank you was to invest a portion of the earnings from my day of hard work into the work of Christ through His church.

I have tithed faithfully ever since, and tithing has been an integral part of my spiritual journey and my most important financial priority. Thankfully, I found a partner, my wife, Ruth, who shares with me the commitment to pass on the importance of tithe to our children and grandchildren. One of our daughters recently received *her* first paycheck—$38.00. We were thrilled when, without any nudging from Ruth or me, she filled out an envelope in church and whispered, "Four dollars is ten percent of thirty-eight dollars, right?" It is this sort of multi-generational giving legacy that this book strives to encourage.

The stories and concepts within this book are suitable as resources for sermons, personal study, or small group study. Tom has gone out into the world and gathered *real* stories of regular Christians whose lives have been blessed and transformed through faithful tithing. A culture of faithful tithing encourages the development of church members who are not just involved, but *invested* in the ministry and mission of the Church of the Nazarene: to make Christlike disciples in the nations. The hope is that this book will be a blessing to its readers and will recast tithe as a transformative and indispensable part of worship.

Dr. Mark E. Lail, Director
Stewardship Ministries,
Church of the Nazarene

# Acknowledgments

Any project of this scope involves the work and support of others. My journey has been more enjoyable thanks to the participation of many who have provided stories, opinions, input, advice, and general support.

Thanks to my friends and colleagues in the Nazarene stewardship office who helped in many ways: Mark E. Lail, my director; Jamie Connally; Deanna Evans; and Josh Jakobitz.

Thanks to those who were willing to share their tithing stories: Angelito Agbuya, Ammie Agbuya, Jeff and Stacey Barker, Mark Brown, Jeff and Peggy Croft, Mike Elliott, Jon Hauser, and Samuel Yangmi.

Also, thanks to those who helped me find these stories: Doug Flemming, Anderson Godoy, David Hayse, and David Phillips.

I am truly grateful for those who took the time to read and critique my manuscript: Jeff Barker, Ben Felder, Rick Garmon, and Rob Kazee. And thanks to the excellent team at Beacon Hill Press for guiding this project to completion.

And, of course, thanks to my wife, Marla, for being a sounding board for my ideas, testing my theories, and trying out formats.

# Introduction

I started this project by asking people to tell me their tithing stories. I asked friends, I asked co-workers, and I asked people who know people. I tried to cast the net as widely as possible. I was curious about the response I would get.

The response was wonderful. I was amazed at how eager so many were to share the story of their tithing journey. Tithing is a very personal thing to many people. It revolves around money and giving money, and a lot of people don't like to talk publicly about those things; most of those who responded would not have talked about it if not for my request. They weren't trying to brag or boast about how spiritual they are. They were excited, because they had an exciting story to tell.

The people I talked with learned about tithing in different ways. Many said they learned about it when they were children and their parents insisted that they set aside a tenth of their allowance or gifts of money they received. Others learned later in life through a pastor's sermon or the advice of a spiritual mentor.

But the stories all shared some common themes.

Most I spoke with described times of crisis when they had to affirm their commitment to tithe in the face of difficulty. In some cases it was as simple as fitting the tithe into a budget that was already stretched beyond limits. In other cases it involved deciding to continue tithing when facing hard financial circumstances.

One exciting theme was repeated over and over in all the stories. Without fail, the storytellers always finished their narratives by talking about how much God had blessed them. It's important to point out that none of these people are millionaires. Some have comfortable lives with nice homes and newer cars; others live more modestly. None, however, live what we would call extravagant lives.

The blessings they were talking about were much deeper than monetary return. These blessings involved physical healing and protection from harm. They involved children growing up in homes where tithing was a way of life and going on to be generous givers themselves. They involved miracles just when miracles were needed.

The people I talked to didn't want to brag, though, and the notion that some people might find their stories boastful is probably what keeps them from sharing their stories more readily. But when asked, these storytellers eagerly shared their exciting experiences.

There were stories from people like Mike. As a child, Mike had severe asthma, and the medicine was expensive. After becoming Christians, his parents felt challenged to tithe, but the cost of his asthma medication was a huge issue. They made the decision to trust God and began to tithe. Soon afterward, Mike's asthma disappeared and has never returned. Mike is a pastor now and joyfully preaches on tithing, because he knows God is faithful. He is reminded every time he takes a deep breath that God honors those who obey Him.

I learned Mark's story through a third party. Mark, the vice-president of a publishing house, grew up knowing that tithing was a priority, but one summer while he was in college, he found himself failing to set aside his tithe. In his mind he had a good reason for not tithing—he wanted to have enough money to go through the next school year without having to work. However, he struggled with his decision and ultimately decided to make up for the tithe he had been holding back. He wrote a check for the full amount and put it into the offering plate.

Several days later, while going through some papers, Mark found a paycheck that he had failed to cash. The amount of the paycheck happened to be just a few dollars more than the check he had written for his tithe!

As it turned out, Mark did have to get a job to help meet expenses during the following school year, but God was faithful to him then and has been faithful to him since. And Mark has been faithful to tithe.

Jeff and Peggy learned about the importance of tithing as children, so when they grew up and got married, it was a given that they would tithe as a couple. As with most people, it wasn't always easy. They made the decision early in their marriage that Peggy would be a stay-at-home mom when they had children, and this made tithing even more difficult. They endured quite a few lean years as they lived on one income, including many years in the ministry. But they remained faithful.

How do Jeff and Peggy describe God's blessings? "We did not get rich, and we are not wealthy," Jeff said, "but God has always been faithful." Peggy talks about God's blessings revealed in their children who were able to attend college and now work in ministry themselves.

"God and His ways are first," she says. "He will supply all our needs."

Mike, Mark, Jeff, and Peggy were eager to tell their stories because they want to give God credit. For them, tithing is not something to be dreaded. It has become a privilege and a way of life. You will also read stories from others—Jeff and Stacey, Angelito and Ammie, Maria, and Jon and his grandmother Sadie. These are stories of faith, and they are testimonies of God's faithfulness.

As exciting as these stories of people who have been faithful to give their tithe are, this book needed to go beyond stories. It's important to know what the Bible says about tithing. Where did this practice come from? What did Jesus and others in the New Testament say about tithing?

There is a danger for those of us who learn about tithing early in our lives—that it might become rote or routine. It becomes so familiar and normal that we fail to remind ourselves why we do it. We fail to stop and consider the impact our faithfulness to tithing has on our lives. I have to admit that I have written tithing checks time after time and dropped them into the offering as a matter of habit. Even though I know God has blessed us and honored us for tithing, I have missed out on so much because of my casual attitude.

I also must admit that sometimes there is a slight hesitation when I write the tithe check. I think of a big bill coming due that week, or I wonder if we can afford to fix the car or pay the mortgage on time. I'm sure many people have these kinds of thoughts that tend to creep in when it's time to tithe.

This journey has taught me, though, that there are several basic principles behind the issue of tithing. These principles are more than just guides or rules. These principles give life to the act of tithing. They give it texture and meaning.

These are principles of ownership and dependence. They are principles that undergird our faith in more ways than giving money to the church. They are principles that remind us not only that God is in charge but also that He is committed to caring for us.

They are principles of practicality. When you think about it, God has provided an ingenious plan for the support of the Church. In the Old Testament world the tithe provided support for the Levites and priests so they could do their work. Even today, tithes provide a way for local churches to do ministry in their communities and around the world. It doesn't matter whether the church exists in an agricultural community or a modern city—the tithe is sufficient for supporting the local congregation.

These principles stand on the promises and mandates of Scripture. Like David, I can acknowledge that God owns everything. Like Abram, I can give my tithe as a symbol that I depend on God. I hear the words of Moses and know that the tithe is holy and an act of worship. Malachi's words challenge me to bring the tithes into the storehouse, reinforcing that the tithe is God's plan for supporting the Church.

And through the words of Malachi and Jesus I am reminded that when I obey God and tithe, God will pour out blessings on my life.

My prayer is that tithing can become more to you than it is now. My hope is that through a renewed commitment to tithing, you will discover the joy of living a generous life.

# The Principle of Ownership

Who am I, and who are my people, that we should be able to give as generously as this? Everything comes from you, and we have given you only what comes from your hand.

—1 Chronicles 29:14

When we give to God, we are just taking our hands off what already belongs to Him.

—Anonymous

It's amazing how easily toddlers learn to emphatically announce, "Mine!" For some reason it's one of the first words in a child's vocabulary. And it's not just a word—it's an attitude, the attitude that what you have belongs to me.

The struggle over ownership begins early. Before we learn to walk or dress ourselves, we learn that if we want it, it's ours. Then we spend the rest of our lives chasing *stuff*. Sometimes it seems that our whole existence is built around getting more for ourselves and keeping others from taking it.

## It All Belongs to God

The idea of ownership is at the very heart of stewardship and, more specifically, the issue of tithing. In order to be a true steward of all God has given us, we must recognize that everything we have belongs to Him in the first place. To give cheerfully requires us to have an adequate understanding that what we are giving doesn't really belong to us anyway—it belongs to God.

David sums it up very well in Psalm 24:1— "The earth is the LORD's, and everything in it, the world, and all who live in it." There is nothing that exists that doesn't already belong to God. It is all His, and our tithe is merely a way of recognizing that fact.

David expressed the same conviction in his prayer in 1 Chronicles 29. In his last days as king, David had initiated a capital campaign to raise funds to build the Temple. The building of the Temple was a life dream—a dream directly from God. David had many successes in his reign, but the one driving force was to build this place of worship in Jerusalem. David had the plans and details ready to go, but it was God's plan that Solomon, David's son, build the Temple.

Still, David was passionate about the project and started the campaign by putting in a large offering of his own gold and silver. The people responded in kind with their own offerings. He watched with pride as tribal leaders and government officials came forward with gifts of gold, silver, bronze, iron, and precious stones. Army commanders and generals followed with their own offerings. The offering turned into a celebration as David and his people rejoiced at the response.

David could easily have patted himself on the back and bragged about his leadership in this endeavor. But he didn't. David understood what was happening and put the accolades where they belonged, at the feet of God. In his usual poetic fashion, he praised God for the generosity of the people while recognizing the source of that generosity.

"Everything in heaven and earth is yours," David said in his prayer to God. "Wealth and honor come from you" (1 Chronicles 29:11-12).

David understood the basic principle of giving to God—it all belongs to God in the first place. Yes, he gave a large part of his fortune to this project, but everything he gave already belonged to God. And yes, the people responded with outstanding generosity, but they only responded with what was already God's.

David summed it up in verse 14: "Who am I, and who are my people, that we should be able to give as generously as this?"

Once we understand that everything we have comes from God and belongs to Him, the whole issue of stewardship takes on a new light. It is not a matter of giving up what belongs to me. Stewardship is managing God's resources and using those resources to build His kingdom. Generosity is not measured against what someone else gives. It is rooted in our understanding of God's ownership of all that we have and our willingness to let go and let God use our resources as He sees fit.

Zig Ziglar, the popular motivational speaker, tells the story of a farmer who sat listening to a sermon on tithing. The preacher talked about how God owned everything, but the farmer disagreed.

After the service, the farmer invited the preacher out to his farm for dinner. Following the meal, the farmer and the preacher took a walk outside. The farmer made a point of showing the preacher around his place. He showed him his house, barn, tool shed, and finished by pointing out his crops. Then he asked the preacher, "I've worked all my life on this land. Do you mean to tell me that it's not my land, but it's the Lord's land?"

The preacher thought about this for a moment and then responded. "Ask me the same question a hundred years from now."

For many people, tithing is an exercise of guilt and calculation. "Can I afford to give ten percent this week?" "Do I have to give ten percent of my net or gross pay?" "If I put this check in the offering, can I pay my bills this week?"

Or we resort back to our toddler-like selfishness. "I worked hard for this." "I built this with my own hands." "I deserve to spend this money on myself."

Recognizing God's ownership of all that we have removes these obstacles and opens the way for generosity. If we can really accept that God already owns it and that it's not ours, it should be easier to give God a percentage as a way of saying to Him, "It's all yours."

The great thing about God's ownership is the freedom it brings. When God owns everything, He is responsible. We are just managers. Our only task is to take care of what He has given us. He provides.

Jesus reminds us that when we try to take ownership for ourselves, things will not end well. What we possess is only temporary. It will not last forever.

"Do not store up for yourselves treasures on earth, where moth and rust destroy, and where thieves break in and steal," Jesus said. "But store up for yourselves treasures in heaven, where moth and rust do not destroy, and where thieves do not break in and steal. For where your treasure is, there your heart will be also" (Matthew 6:19-21).

On the other hand, when we accept God's ownership and remove our hands from it, He promises to take care of things. Jesus follows with these words:

Therefore I tell you, do not worry about your life, what you will eat or drink; or about your body, what you will wear. Is not life more important than food, and the body more important than clothes? Look at the birds of the air; they do not sow or reap or store away in barns, and yet your heavenly Father feeds them. Are you not much more valuable than they? Who of you by worrying can add a single hour to his life?

And why do you worry about clothes? See how the lilies of the field grow. They do not labor or spin. Yet I tell you that not even Solomon in all his splendor was dressed like one of these. If that is how God clothes the grass of the field, which is here today and tomorrow is thrown into the fire, will he not much more clothe you, O you of little faith? So do not worry, saying, "What shall we eat?" or "What shall we drink?" or "What shall we wear?" For the pagans run after all these things, and your heavenly Father knows that you need them (Matthew 6:25-32).

Between my junior and senior years in college, a friend from church asked me to house-sit while he and his family were on vacation. They would be gone for about three weeks, and I would have access to the house and everything in it during that time. Three weeks in a nice house by the lake was a much better option than the dorm room, so I accepted.

For those three weeks I lived in his house. I swam in his pool. I ate the food in his fridge. I watched his nice television. I had access to everything in that house.

But the house was not mine. When he returned I had no right to bolt the door and yell, "It's mine now!" The house belonged to him, and when it was time to move out, I did. He was the owner. I was just the caretaker for a little while.

It was a fun three weeks. I knew all along, though, that this was not my house. I was just there to take care of it for the owner. Everything in the house belonged to the owner, not me.

Years later, my wife and I bought our first house. It was exciting. Finally we had a house that belonged to us. No more landlord to tell us whether or not we could paint the living room. We could paint any room any color whenever we wanted. We could decorate any way we wanted. We could take a wall out if we wanted to.

But it didn't take long for us to realize there is a dark side to home ownership. When the plumbing backs up, I have to fix it or, more likely, pay someone else to fix it. I am responsible for the leak in the roof, and I have to pay the insurance. I have to make sure the house is cared for. I have to take care of all those things because, in earthly terms, I am the owner.

Acknowledging God's ownership of our belongings is liberating. I don't have to worry about stuff. I don't have to wonder how I am going to fix problems, because I can trust God, the owner, to help me and to take care of me.

I don't have to hold tightly to my stuff and cry, "It's mine!" I don't have to worry that I might starve if I pay my tithe. I can trust God to be faithful, just as He has promised He would be. Instead of grabbing, I can hold my hands out and say, "It's yours."

## Grandma Sadie and the Social Worker

Jon pastors a growing, exciting church in Fargo, North Dakota. Even though some pastors find it hard to preach or talk about tithing, it's not a subject Jon shies away from.

"Jesus loved the rich young ruler enough to talk to him about money," Jon says. "If I love my people, I will do the same."

Jon credits tithing for saving his marriage and his ministry. As a seminary student, he found it difficult to pay his tithe, and he tried to justify not paying it. "I looked at it like this," Jon said. "I was studying for the ministry and giving up a lucrative career as an engineer to do it. The way I saw it, I was already sacrificing."

But the lesson Jon learned was that *he* wasn't giving up anything. God owned it all, including his future.

Jon learned most of his lessons on tithing from his parents and grandmother. "My mom made me tithe," Jon says. "I didn't like it then, but now I am so thankful she did."

Jon grew up hearing the story of his grandmother's experience with tithing. Grandma Sadie didn't have much in her life. Her husband left her and their three little girls when she was a young mother. She survived by cleaning houses and offices in the small town of Williston, North Dakota.

One day, at the urging of one of her daughters, Sadie attended a little church in her town, and for the first time she heard the gospel. She responded and allowed Christ to take possession of her. She quickly immersed herself in the Bible and learned what it meant to follow Christ.

One of the early lessons she learned is that God owns everything but asks for only ten percent in return—the tithe. Even on her small income she began to tithe, and she made it a lifelong habit.

Years later, the girls had grown up and moved away, and Sadie was living alone. She was still making a living as best she could, but age and health had made it more difficult. She could not earn enough to survive. One day a government social worker came to visit and help her get assistance. After the social worker totaled all the expenses, she told Sadie the amount she would be getting from the government. Sadie suddenly remembered that she had failed to include enough for tithe.

"The government doesn't pay tithe," the social worker responded. "And there's not enough here for you to give any to the church."

Sadie and the social worker went back and forth on the issue. Sadie insisted that she was going to pay her tithe even if it meant going without something. The social worker continued to point out that there wasn't enough money to do that. Finally, the social worker gave in and added enough money to Sadie's assistance for her to pay tithe.

The matter was really very clear for Sadie. She didn't own it, and the government didn't own it. Paying her tithe was a way to express God's ownership and her dependence on Him.

## Your Ownership Story

Write about something you possess that's very important to you. How did you get it? Why is it important?

_____

_____

_____

_____

_____

_____

_____

_____

_____

_____

_____

_____

_____

_____

_____

_____

_____

## ■ Think

1. Write down the items you personally own. Don't try to be super-spiritual here. What are the things you own in "earthly" terms?

_____

_____

_____

_____

_____

2. How can you use these things in a way that shows you understand God is the ultimate owner?

_____

_____

_____

_____

_____

_____

3. Does the fact that God owns it all give you encouragement to tithe? Does it make it easier? Does it make it harder?

_____

_____

_____

_____

_____

_____

4. Are there things in your life you need to re-lease to God? If so, what are they?

_____

_____

_____

_____

_____

_____

_____

## ■ Discover

Read the following verses.

- "To the Lord your God belong the heavens, even the highest heavens, the earth and everything in it" (Deuteronomy 10:14).

- "Is not wisdom found among the aged? Does not long life bring understanding? To God belong wisdom and power; counsel and understanding are his" (Job 12:12-13).

- "If he holds back the waters, there is drought; if he lets them loose, they devastate the land. To him belong strength and victory; both deceived and deceiver are his. He leads counselors away stripped and makes fools of judges" (Job 12:15-17).

- "Declare his glory among the nations, his marvelous deeds among all peoples. For great is the Lord and most worthy of praise; he is to be feared above all gods. For all the gods of the nations are idols, but the Lord made the heavens" (Psalm 96:3-5).

- "Do you not know that your body is a temple of the Holy Spirit, who is in you, whom you have received from God? You are not your own; you were bought at a price. Therefore honor God with your body" (1 Corinthians 6:19-20).

- "By him all things were created: things in heaven and on earth, visible and invisible, whether thrones or powers or rulers or authorities; all things were created by him and for him. He is before all things, and in him all things hold together" (Colossians 1:16-17).

What do these verses say to you about ownership?

_____

_____

_____

_____

_____

_____

_____

# The Principle of Dependence

"Blessed be God Most High, who delivered your enemies into your hand." Then Abram gave him a tenth of everything.
—Genesis 14:20

Giving is more than a responsibility—it is a privilege; more than an act of obedience—it is evidence of our faith.
—William A. Ward

You're rich if you've had a meal today.
—Billy Graham

Megan spent nine days in the hospital. It was a long nine days. For most of the time, her little three-year-old body had tubes inserted just about everywhere you could imagine. Her appendix had burst, and she was filled with an infection. She was a sick little girl.

She was also *my* little girl, and I wanted desperately to do something to help her. But I couldn't. I couldn't take the infection away. I couldn't relieve the pain. I couldn't even give her food or drink when she begged for a drink of water. It was a long time ago, but I still remember how helpless I felt.

In times like this, there's nothing to do but lean on God and trust that He will watch over this little person you love and take care of her. I had to depend on Him to be there.

Most of the time, we can bring ourselves to depend on God when things get serious. Those are the times when we quickly turn to Him and ask for help. Those are the times when we place our faith in Him and trust and hope that He will intervene.

But there are other times when we get into this I-can-fix-it-myself mode and charge full-steam-ahead without any thought of including God. *I'm self-sufficient. I can figure this out. I'm smart. I can fix this. I know best.* Eventually we get to the end of our rope and have to call for God to rescue us.

Recognizing our dependence on God for our existence and sustenance is as important as understanding that God owns everything. We may acknowledge that God owns it all, but our human nature is to be self-dependent. Many of us are very good at feeling as though we can manage most of our lives on our own. We turn to God only when it's clear we're stuck.

## Abram's Tithe

The earliest use of the word *tithe* in Scripture occurs in Genesis 14. Abram paid a tithe to Melchizedek, a priest of God. Abram gave this tithe as a sign of his dependence on God and his gratitude for God's help in recent battles.

Several city-states, each with a king, surrounded Abram in Canaan. Four of these leaders, the kings of Mesopotamia, had exerted control over the region for many years until five of the subjected kings had finally had enough and rebelled. The Mesopotamian kings took this opportunity and led their armies on a full-scale invasion, destroying every city and army that got in their way. But they didn't stop with defeating the armies. Victorious kings also looted the cities, taking whatever they wanted, including citizens. These citizens became slaves for the conquering king.

Abram managed to stay out of the ruckus, at least until the members of his own family were taken as slaves. When the city of Sodom was defeated, the armies took Lot and his family as slaves. Word of this got back to Abram, and he could no longer sit on the sidelines.

Abram gathered his men—about 300 of them—and set off to rescue his family. Along the way Abram and his army defeated the larger armies of the Mesopotamian kings, rescued the slaves, and took back the loot.

The victory party is described in Genesis 14. The gathering took place in the Valley of Shaveh, also known as the Valley of the Kings. Abram and his army attended as did the new king of Sodom. The former king had not survived the war. Melchizedek also attended and directed a worship service in celebration of God's help. It was here that Abram presented Melchizedek with a tithe in recognition of God's provision and help during the battles.

Abram understood that his existence and survival depended on God. When Abram gave the tithe to Melchizedek, he did so in the presence of the king of Sodom, who served other gods. Abram's tithe was more than a personal act of worship and dependence. He also gave the tithe as a public symbol that his God was the one true God. He wanted all in attendance to know that he relied completely on God for everything.

The battles we face before bringing our tithe are usually not as severe as the one Abram faced. But we still bring our tithes to God in the context of showing that our entire existence is dependent on Him. Our income, family, possessions, jobs, toys, investments, and friends are all due to God's provision. Without God we are nothing, and we have nothing. That is true whether we serve Him or not.

Earlier we saw that David understood the concept of ownership and that this was conveyed in his response to the generosity of his people. In 1 Chronicles 29 we also see that David had learned to depend on God. He said,

Who am I, and who are my people, that we should be able to give as generously as this? *(1 Chronicles 29:14).*

David compared us to aliens in a strange land and shadows on the ground. As aliens we are merely borrowing this space for a little while. We didn't build it or create it. God did that. Our task is to take care of this space. God assumes the responsibility of providing what we need to do that.

Giving God our tithe is a perfect outward symbol of our dependence on Him. By its very nature the tithe, as a percentage, represents the whole. The giving of a tenth is a way of saying, "I am giving this percentage to show that God owns 100 percent."

Why do we struggle to tithe? Usually it is because we fear that we can't make it without that ten percent. We are afraid we will need it for bills or emergencies. Or we think we need to hold onto it for things we want. In effect we are saying to God, "Despite what you say, I don't trust you to take care of me if I pay my tithe" or "I can't depend on you."

Brother Andrew, a missionary known for smuggling Bibles to Communist countries during the Cold War era, tells a story of learning to depend on God while tithing. In his book *The Narrow Road* he tells how he and a team of students were sent out on a missionary tour through Scotland. They were given a one-pound note and expected to pay for their own transportation, food, lodging, building rentals, advertising, and any other expenses. And they were expected to give the one-pound note back to the school when they returned.[1]

Hearing this, Andrew joked that they would be taking up offerings all the time. But that was not to be the case. They were given specific instructions that they could not take up any offerings. In fact, they could not tell anyone of their need for money.

Andrew and his team of five other students set out on their four-week mission tour with their one-pound note and their instructions. They followed the instructions, and somehow God provided for their needs. Andrew wrote,

> Later, when I tried to reconstruct where our funds came from during those four weeks, it was hard to. It seemed that what we needed was always just there. Sometimes a letter would arrive from one of the boys' parents with a little money. Sometimes we would get a check in the mail from a church we had

visited. The notes that came with these gifts were always interesting. "I know you don't need the money or you would have mentioned it," someone would write, "but God just wouldn't let me get to sleep tonight until I had put this in an envelope for you."

Andrew and his team stuck to the rule of not collecting money and added one of their own: they committed to tithe on everything they received and to do so as soon as they received it. When the boys returned to school, they were able to pay back the one-pound note and had money left over to send to missions.

It didn't go that way for another student team, however.

Two student teams were sent out by the school at the same time. The other team wasn't as strict about tithing. Andrew wrote,

> They set aside ten percent all right, but they didn't give it away immediately "in case [they] ran into an emergency." Of course they had emergencies! So did we, every day. But they ended their month owing

money to hotels, lecture halls, and markets all over Scotland, while we came back to school almost ten pounds ahead.

## The Tithe Pie

I think most of us look at tithing in one of two ways. One way to view the tithe is as the final ten percent—if ten percent is left. If you look at the tithe this way, you make sure to meet all your financial obligations before paying the tithe. You might also set aside some for savings and emergencies. And, of course, there is fun and entertainment. After all, you deserve it. Then, if anything is left, you give to God.

The second approach is to pay the tithe first. It's the first check you write, or the first ten percent of your earnings. Once the tithe is paid, everything else is dealt with.

These two approaches remind me of two pies. Both pies have many slices that represent all the things we acquire with our wealth. There are slices for rent or mortgage, a car payment or payments, school bills, clothing, shoes, utilities, food, and things like that. Plus, some slices of the pie go for toys and gadgets, vacations, dinners out, and other fun things.

The person with the first pie decides to take slices for all the bills, obligations, and fun stuff first. God then gets whatever remains of the pie. The other person gives God the first slice and then takes care of everything else with the remaining slices.

You see, the person with the second pie understands that this is God's pie. This pie exists only because God provided it. So a tenth of the pie is set aside for God before anyone else is served. Now, thanks to God's blessings, this person still has ninety percent of the pie to use for all the things he or she needs and wants. The remaining portions may not cover all the wants, but the person is confident that his or her needs will be met.

The second pie represents a tither who depends on God for everything. The first pie represents the person who puts everything else before the tithe and, by doing that, shows that he or she can't quite get to the place of depending on God to meet all of his or her needs.

What does your pie look like?

## Maria's Tithe

For Maria, it's simple. God owns everything, and He provides all she needs. By our standards, Maria doesn't have much. She lives in a modest hut in a jungle area of Peru and survives by growing her own food. Each week she walks for an hour to get to church. The 80-year-old travels with her walking stick down into a valley, across uneven terrain, and up another large hill to worship in the village of Shushug in the Amazon region of Peru.

Maria also brings her tithe to church. Unlike most of us, she doesn't bring cash or checks. She brings yucca—an edible root. Maria doesn't work and earn a wage. Her garden provides her food and gives her something to trade for other needs. Her tithe comes from her garden. Before she gathers any food for herself, she gathers ten percent of the crop for her tithe.

Why? Because, in Maria's words, "God owns it all anyway." Maria understands that the food that comes from the ground belongs to God. God provides for her needs, and she is happy to give ten percent of the food to help her little church in the jungles of Peru. Maria has learned to depend on God, and she demonstrates that dependence by bringing her tithe to church each week.

## Your Dependence Story

Write about a time when you had to depend on God. What was the result? What scriptures helped you during this time? What words from friends or family members brought faith or assurance?

_____

_____

_____

_____

_____

_____

_____

_____

_____

_____

_____

_____

_____

_____

# ■ Think

1. When have you had to really depend on God for His help?

_____

_____

_____

_____

_____

_____

2. What type of problems do you try to fix on your own before finally realizing you need God's help?

_____

_____

_____

_____

_____

_____

_____

3. In what areas of your life do you find it most difficult to trust God?

_____

_____

_____

_____

_____

_____

_____

4. How difficult is it to depend on God to help you in financial situations? How does this affect your tithe?

_____

_____

_____

_____

_____

_____

_____

## ■ Discover

Read the following verses.

- "He alone is my rock and my salvation; he is my fortress, I will not be shaken. My salvation and my honor depend on God; he is my mighty rock, my refuge" (Psalm 62:6-7).

- "Now I know that the LORD saves his anointed; he answers him from his holy heaven with the saving power of his right hand. Some trust in chariots and some in horses, but we trust in the name of the LORD our God. They are brought to their knees and fall, but we rise up and stand firm" (Psalm 20:6-8).

- "Trust in the LORD with all your heart and lean not on your own understanding; in all your ways acknowledge him, and he will make your paths straight" (Proverbs 3:5-6).

- "He says to Moses, 'I will have mercy on whom I have mercy, and I will have compassion on whom I have compassion.' It does not, therefore, depend on man's desire or effort, but on God's mercy. For the Scripture says to Pharaoh: 'I raised you up for this very purpose, that I might display my power in you and that my name might be proclaimed in all the earth'" (Romans 9:15-17).

What do these verses say to you about your dependence on God?

_____

_____

_____

_____

_____

_____

_____

_____

_____

_____

_____

# The Principle of Worship

A tithe of everything from the land, whether grain from the soil or fruit from the trees, belongs to the LORD; it is holy to the LORD.

—Leviticus 27:30

The worship that is empty handed is simply not worship at all. The bringing of an offering to God is pictured in the Scripture as a high and inestimable part of worship. —Ralph S. Cushman

It's hard to wrap our heads around the way Hebrews worshiped in Old Testament times. So many aspects of their worship are foreign to us. Perhaps the most foreign is the sacrificial system. It's a system far removed from how we worship today.

However, it's not hard to understand that these people came to worship. The system required a certain amount of preparation. They couldn't just jump on a donkey and take off for church. They had to get ready to worship.

The worship was also unique in that it involved all the senses—sight, sound, smell, touch, and taste. Because of this, the worshiper had to be engaged on different levels. Every breath, every look, every sound called the Hebrews to worship.

*The smell of the sacrifices hits you before you even set foot on the Temple property.*

*But immediately your eyes are engaged in the Temple experience, and you are in awe of the grandeur of God's house. You have been here before, but this is a place designed to elicit amazement on every visit. As you wander through the Temple area, other sights and colors explode before your eyes: the beautiful drapes and coverings decorated in gold and the rich fabrics that formed the wardrobe of the priests with their many colors and patterns.*

*The sounds of the Temple area are both loud and beautiful. The conversation and laughter of many people gathering in one place fills the air. There is the sound of horns calling the people to worship and other instruments finding the proper tune and note. And, of course, there are the chants and cries of the religious leaders, calling everyone to a place of worship and lifting prayers to God.*

The ceremonies involved the sharing of food and drink brought for the festivals. Together the people ate and drank and shared stories.

The act of giving was a central part of the worship experience. This is when the people brought their tithe to the Lord. As people of the

land, this tithe came in the form of crops and animals. If they came from too far away to trans-
port their own crops and animals, there was a
system for that. Everyone brought an offering
that reflected how God had blessed them. The
tithe and worship were as interwoven as the col-
orful threads on the priestly garments.

The tithe was designed to be part of our worship of God. The law specified that it was to be
brought at these times of worship and celebration. And the tithe was declared holy. As Leviticus 27:30 says, "It [the tithe] is holy to the LORD."

Maybe I am more visual, but it is easier for
me to match tithing and worship in the Old Testament context than in current worship services.
The sights and sounds of biblical worship add
to the ambience and mystery of the whole experience. The worshiper is engaged on every level. I think it would be easier to feel that my tithe
was an act of worship in that setting. It would
be easier to understand that my tithe was holy.

Changes in culture make it important for us
to be intentional about our tithes. Somehow that

sense of holiness is lost when I pay my tithe by check or through an online funds transfer. Of course, this still represents a tenth, hopefully the first tenth, but it's different. I don't think it's wrong to tithe by check or bank transfer, but it does force me to work harder to make the tithe a worship experience.

As it says in Leviticus, the tithe is holy. That sets it apart and makes it different from everything else. It makes it special and unique. And it makes it special to God. So how do I make sure that my tithe is given in a way that is holy and worshipful?

## A Matter of Attitude

The way you bring your tithe is a matter of attitude. We don't tithe because God needs our money. He owns it all. He created everything. Truthfully, God doesn't need anything we possess.

So the act of bringing God a big tithe check does not impress Him. It doesn't make God turn to the heavenly treasurer and say, "Hey, look—we can pay the bills now!"

What impresses God is my *attitude* when I tithe.

The story of Cain and Abel is a case study in good and bad attitudes when giving offerings to God. Their story is in Genesis 4. It's a short story, and it doesn't have a happy ending.

Cain, the firstborn son of Adam and Eve, was a farmer like his dad. He grew crops. His brother, Abel, raised animals, perhaps sheep or goats. Even in those early days, worship was part of the regular schedule. And the offering was a part of worship.

When it came time to worship God, the two brothers brought their offerings to God. They did as you would expect. Cain grabbed some crops from the field and Abel brought an animal. But something was wrong. God was pleased with Abel's offering and accepted it gladly. But he rejected Cain's offering. It wasn't acceptable.

Why?

The clues point to attitude. In Genesis 4:4 we read that "Abel brought fat portions from some of the firstborn of his flock." Compare this with verse 3 that says that Cain "brought some of the fruits of the soil."

There is a contrast in attitudes based on how the brothers chose and brought their offering. Cain was casual in his approach to the offering, just grabbing some of the crops he grew. Meanwhile, Abel came to worship with a different attitude. He brought the best part of some of his firstborn animals.

The idea of "first things" is closely related to the concept of the tenth. In fact, the idea of giving your tithe as the first tenth is directly related to bringing the first or best.

Throughout the Old Testament, discussions of offerings for God focus a lot on bringing the best—or the first. Often, rather than leaving the choice of offering to the giver, God asks specifically for the first, which represents the best. In Abel's case, there is something superior and more significant about sacrificing the firstborn of his flock.

In Numbers 18, God describes to Aaron how the offerings are to be shared with the priests. These offerings were described as "the most holy."

I give you all the finest olive oil and all the finest new wine and grain they give the LORD as the firstfruits of their harvest. All the land's firstfruits that they bring to the LORD will be yours (Numbers 18:12-13).

When Hezekiah became king at the age of twenty-five, he inherited a kingdom that had become very casual in its worship and offerings. The Temple was defiled. The people turned away from God. Eventually the Temple was shut.

One of Hezekiah's first acts was to clean up the Temple and open it back up. He called the Levites and priests together and re-commissioned them for service. He called on the people to bring their offerings to support the Levites and priests so they could focus on Temple duties.

As soon as the order went out, the Israelites generously gave the firstfruits of their grain, new wine, oil and honey and all that the fields produced. They brought a great amount, a tithe of everything. The men of

Israel and Judah who lived in the towns of Judah also brought a tithe of their herds and flocks and a tithe of the holy things dedicated to the LORD their God, and they piled them in heaps *(2 Chronicles 31:5-6)*.

A key to the revival of God's people under the leadership of Hezekiah was their change of attitude. They changed the way they approached worship. In turn, they changed their ungodly actions.

## God Loves a Cheerful Giver

Paul addressed the relationship between attitude and giving in his second letter to the Corinthians. The Corinthian church had volunteered to give an offering to help the mother church in Jerusalem. However, it was taking a while for the Corinthians to raise this offering, and Paul sensed that the excitement was waning. He wanted to make sure that the church was still on board. He also wanted to make sure they were giving for the right reasons.

One of Paul's concerns was the attitude of the Corinthians. He wanted the gift to be a generous one instead of an offering given "grudgingly" (2 Corinthians 9:5). He reminded them that the decision to give should not be done "reluctantly or under compulsion." Why? Because "God loves a cheerful giver" (2 Corinthians 9:7).

In his plea to the Corinthians, Paul contrasted their situation with that of the newer church in Macedonia. When the Macedonian Christians heard about the need in Jerusalem, they responded just like the Corinthians and took an offering. However, the Macedonians were facing hardship and poverty. Perhaps they weren't able to give as much as the Corinthians, but they gave what they could. In fact, despite their hardships, they pleaded for the opportunity to participate in this offering.

Paul proudly describes the generosity of these new Christians in Macedonia. Out of their hardship and extreme poverty Paul says they gave with "overflowing joy" and entirely on their own without prompting from anyone else (2 Corinthians 8:2-3).

The amount wasn't important. They gave with joy rather than because they felt obligated. While their total may not have matched that of the Corinthians, the Macedonians gave generously. Paul praised them for their attitude. The bottom line is that when we give with the right attitude, the need will be met because of our generosity.

## Tithing with a Heart for Others

The one time Jesus mentions the tithe, He does so while calling out the religious leaders of the day for their bad attitudes.

Woe to you, teachers of the law and Pharisees, you hypocrites! You give a tenth of your spices—mint, dill and cumin. But you have neglected the more important matters of the law—justice, mercy and faithfulness. You should have practiced the latter, without neglecting the former *(Matthew 23:23)*.

The religious people and leaders of Jesus' day were a proud bunch. They were proud of how "holy" and "spiritual" they were and were very willing to show it. They were so proud that the race to be seen as the most holy became more important than the reason for giving.

Jesus reprimanded the leaders for being so proud of their practice of tithing but failing to show justice and mercy to those in need. He pointed out the irony. The Pharisees were regular in their tithe, but only as a matter of pride. At the same time, all around them people were in need. The pride of these religious leaders was like a blindfold that kept them from seeing the hurt and pain around them.

The point Jesus made was that, while the act of tithing was right and to be commended, the attitude cannot be ignored. In this case, the attitude was one of arrogance and pride. And because of this wrong attitude, the religious leaders were unable to see and respond to the needs of orphans, widows, prisoners, immigrants, and others. It is difficult to see the downtrodden when your nose is up in the air with pride.

Jesus was not adding a new component to Kingdom living. Read what the Old Testament said about the tithe:

> At the end of every three years, bring all the tithes of that year's produce and store it in your towns, so that the Levites (who have no allotment or inheritance of their own) and the aliens, the fatherless and the widows who live in your towns may come and eat and be satisfied, and so that the LORD your God may bless you in all the work of your hands *(Deuteronomy 14:28-29)*.

The same concept is repeated in Deuteronomy 26:

> When you have finished setting aside a tenth of all your produce in the third year, the year of the tithe, you shall give it to the Levite, the alien, the fatherless and the widow, so that they may eat in your towns and be satisfied *(Deuteronomy 26:12)*.

As a holy offering to God, our hearts are to be in the right place when we bring the tithe. As a community of faith, we dedicate our tithe to helping those who need the help. There is nothing wrong with building great sanctuaries. There is nothing wrong with funding unique and creative ministries. But in doing so, are we forgetting those who were intended as recipients of at least part of our tithe?

Attitude goes beyond smiling while putting an offering into the basket or plate. A proper tithing attitude calls all of us to recognize the needs around us. We can't forget that God's tithing plan provided both for the work of the Temple and the needs of others such as widows and orphans, the hungry and homeless, the prisoner and the stranger.

## The Tithing Challenge

A group of Christians among the Lahu people in Thailand has discovered the power of tithing to excite and grow a church. Samuel, the district superintendent of a group of churches in northern Thailand, challenged the members of his district churches to tithe, but they responded, "We have no money."

So Samuel began to train his pastors and insist that tithing be taught as a part of membership classes. It has taken some time, but the Lahu members are beginning to understand that tithing is one aspect of being in this community of believers.

"Today the Lahu people take tithing very seriously," Samuel said. "In our strongest churches, eighty-five percent of the members tithe."

The result? Most of the churches now support their pastor with a regular salary. The people give regularly to missions offerings and assist local students with money for Bible college. They also sponsor an annual family camp and send members to start new churches.

"The more they give to God, the more God blesses them," Samuel said. "We see no turning back for the Lahu people. God is blessing them because of their faithfulness in tithing."

## Your Worship Story

Describe your normal tithing experience. What senses are involved? What do you see and hear? What do you smell and taste? What do you feel?

_____

_____

_____

_____

_____

_____

_____

_____

_____

_____

_____

_____

_____

_____

_____

_____

# ■ Think

1. Does your church make the giving of tithe and offerings a part of worship? If so, how?

_____

_____

_____

_____

_____

_____

_____

2. What is your attitude when you bring your tithe? Are you cheerful? Do you tithe grudgingly?

_____

_____

_____

_____

_____

_____

3. What could be done to make giving tithes and offerings in your church a more worshipful experience? What would help you approach this time with an attitude of worship?

_____

_____

_____

_____

_____

_____

_____

4. What are the real needs of people in your faith community? How is your tithe being used to meet those needs?

_____

_____

_____

_____

_____

_____

_____

# ■ Discover

Read the following accounts of worship and giving.

- "Ascribe to the LORD, O families of nations, ascribe to the LORD glory and strength, ascribe to the LORD the glory due his name. Bring an offering and come before him; worship the LORD in the splendor of his holiness. Tremble before him, all the earth! The world is firmly established; it cannot be moved" (1 Chronicles 16:28-30).

- "Hezekiah gave the order to sacrifice the burnt offering on the altar. As the offering began, singing to the LORD began also, accompanied by trumpets and the instruments of David king of Israel. The whole assembly bowed in worship, while the singers sang and the trumpeters played. All this continued until the sacrifice of the burnt offering was completed. When the offerings were finished, the king and everyone present with him knelt down and worshiped" (2 Chronicles 29:27-29).

- "Hezekiah assigned the priests and Levites to divisions—each of them according to their duties as priests or Levites—to offer burnt offerings and fellowship offerings, to minister, to give thanks and to sing praises at the gates of the LORD's dwelling. The king contributed from his own possessions for the morning and evening burnt offerings and for the burnt offerings on the Sabbaths, New Moons and appointed feasts as written in the Law of the LORD" (2 Chronicles 31:2-3).

What senses were involved? What did they see, hear, smell, taste, or touch?

_____

_____

_____

_____

_____

_____

# The Principle of Church Support

Do not neglect the Levites living in your towns,
for they have no allotment or inheritance of their
own.                                   —Deuteronomy 14:27


On the first day of every week, each one of you
should set aside a sum of money in keeping with
his income, saving it up, so that when I come no
collections will have to be made.
                                       —1 Corinthians 16:2


No church ever has a money problem, only a
faithfulness problem.                  —Brian Kluth

Let's be clear: God doesn't need our money. God owns everything already. God is the Creator. If you put those three realities together, it's obvious that God doesn't need anything you or I could ever give Him.

But in instituting the tithe, God has created a system for the ongoing support of the Church. When we honor Him by giving our tithe, we also make it possible for pastors to preach the gospel, missionaries to tell people about Jesus, and churches to feed the hungry and help those who are in need. The tithe is God's economic plan for mission support.

From the time the tithe was instituted as law, it was intended for the support of those who provided ministry. In setting up a society structure, Israel was divided into twelve tribes. When they reached the Promised Land, each of the tribes, except the Levites, received a portion of land to live on, farm, and manage. The Levites, as the caretakers of the Temple, did not receive land, which meant they had no tangible means of providing for their own support.

The solution was the tithe. Each of the other eleven tribes brought their tithe to the Temple to be used to support the Levites and the ministry of the Temple. God told Moses, "I have taken the Levites from among the Israelites in place of the first male offspring of every Israelite woman. The Levites are mine, for all the firstborn are mine" (Numbers 3:12-13).

Later, in giving specific instructions for the tithe, the people were instructed to bring their tithes and not forget the Levites "For they have no allotment or inheritance of their own" (Deuteronomy 14:27). The tithe was used to support those who were called by God to minister to the people.

In Nehemiah 10 the people were reminded of the importance of the tithe to the support of the house of God. They were to bring the tithes to the Levites, and the Levites themselves were expected to tithe. "We will not neglect the house of our God," said Nehemiah (Nehemiah 10:39). Later, in Nehemiah 13, he describes the chamber—or storehouse—that was built specifically to hold these offerings.

Israel, unfortunately, didn't always live up to this command. We find that years later the people had become casual and lackluster in their giving. Because of this, a budget problem developed, and the Levites had to find other ways of supporting themselves. In turn, the ministry of the Temple suffered.

This is the situation that Malachi confronted. "Will a man rob God?" he asked the people. Of course, the people pretended to be unaware of what he was talking about. "How do we rob God?" they asked. Malachi's response: "In tithes and offerings" (Malachi 3:8). And Malachi urged them to bring the whole tithe into the storehouse of the Temple "that there may be food in [God's] house" (Malachi 3:10).

When God's people tithe, God's economy works. There is money for the work of the church and money to pay a pastor a living wage. When God's people tithe, God's Church is able to fulfill its mission in the world.

Many people like to argue that the church is always asking for money. In fact, this has become an excuse for some people to avoid attending church. The truth is, yes, churches do take offerings. After all, we live in a cash economy. It takes money to keep the lights on and the air conditioning running. It takes money to support the pastor and staff. It takes money to buy books and materials. The need of money is a reality of life.

Let's be clear, though. When we represent God, we don't have to beg for money. Remember—God doesn't need our money. He has provided a way for His Church to survive in any age and in any economy. As a tenth, the tithe is always based on the current economy and works with the local currency.

That doesn't mean there won't be shortfalls. It doesn't mean all pastors can work full time. And it doesn't mean every church can pay all the bills and keep the lights on. But that has nothing to do with God. It has everything to do with you and me. It has to do with the fact that many Christians don't tithe.

Recent surveys in the United States show that fewer than ten percent of Christian households tithe. Among those who consider themselves born-again Christians, the number is still low: fourteen percent.[1] That is eighty-five to ninety percent below where it should be if we followed God's plan. Look at it this way: can you imagine if next year your church received ten times as much as it received this year? Could your church pay a decent wage to the pastor? Could you do the kind of ministry in the community that you long to do? Could you provide a higher level of support to global missions? Of course you could.

## Is the Tithe Still Valid?

While we're talking about current issues, let's deal with a significant argument among Christians. Is the tithe still valid? Or is it, as some would argue, outdated and no longer required by Scripture? In general, the argument is that the tithe is an Old Testament idea and concept and that we are living under New Testament guidelines. Some also argue that Jesus didn't promote tithing.

Yes, tithing is an Old Testament law or concept, and it is true that we no longer live under the Mosaic Law. However, there is no reason for the tithe to have been deleted as a spiritual discipline for today's Christian. If nothing else, the principles discussed in this book remind us that tithing is foundational to all Christian giving.

Some argue that Jesus didn't promote or endorse tithing. Yet those who make this argument fail to look closely at the Scriptures.

In Jesus' main discourse related to tithing, He chastises the Pharisees for their lack of justice and mercy. "Woe to you, teachers of the law and Pharisees, you hypocrites! You give a tenth of your spices—mint, dill and cumin. But you have neglected the more important matters of the law—justice, mercy and faithfulness. You should have practiced the latter, without neglecting the former" (Matthew 23:23).

Jesus calls the teachers and Pharisees hypocrites because they follow the law, including tithing, but fail to exhibit other Kingdom attributes like showing justice and mercy to those who need it. Jesus never said tithing was not required. In fact, He actually commended them for tithing, saying that this is what they should be doing. The problem was that they publicly and proudly followed the letter of the law on things like tithing and ignored the spirit and intent of the law on other issues.

In his book *Stewards of God,* Milo Kauffman uses the following logic against those who claim Jesus didn't endorse tithing.

1. By the time Jesus was born, tithing was well established, and Jesus was brought up in a Jewish home with Jewish training.
2. Jesus made it clear that He came to fulfill the law, not abolish it (Matthew 5:17).
3. In all other ways Jesus observed Jewish tradition.

4. The Pharisees tried every kind of accusation against Jesus in order to discredit Him, but they never accused Him of failing to tithe.

5. Jesus' standard was always higher than the law, not lower (Matthew 5:17-48).[2]

In one of the best resources on the subject of tithing, *The Tithe in Scripture*, Henry Lansdell agrees with this line of thought. He says that we must acknowledge that "tithe-paying was enjoined upon the Jews, by God, in the law; and we all contend that Jesus Christ, as a Jew, kept that law to the letter." Therefore, Lansdell continues, "The inference seems inevitable that the Lord Jesus himself paid tithes."[3]

So the real issue is not whether or not a Christian should tithe but whether or not a Christian should give *beyond* the tithe. After all, Jesus challenged His followers to generosity.

"Jesus not only endorsed the tithe but went beyond the tithe in His endorsement," Kauffman said. "Tithes were not types like sacrifices and the Sabbath, which were fulfilled and replaced by something better, nor, like circumcision, was it declared unnecessary. The only valid argument against the tithe for the Christian is the argument 'beyond the tithe.'"[4]

Yes, when it comes to tithing, the New Testament teaching of Jesus does trump Old Testament regulations. But the teachings of Jesus do not relieve the Christian of the responsibility to give a tenth. Rather, they call on the Christian to go beyond the ten percent and be generous givers.

If Christians gave just a tenth, there would be plenty of support for the ministries of the church. Imagine what God's people could do if all Christians went beyond the tithe and gave generously as God directed.

## An Act of Community

When Christians tithe to the local church, they also participate in community. In the early days of the Church we read that the "believers were together and had everything in common" (Acts 2:44). They sold their possessions and goods to help those in need. The act of gathering and sharing built this early community. It bonded these new believers to each other and opened their eyes to each other's needs.

This description of the early days of the Church represented more than just tithing. But the act of tithing to the local church has the effect of building a community. The commitment to tithing represents a commitment to that local congregation. It's an investment in the ministry of that local church. Investors naturally have a greater stake in what happens. They pay more attention. They participate more. They care more.

Evangelist Bailey Smith preaches this connection between tithing and community.

If you are not a tither or a giver to the Lord and you start giving, I promise that you'll love the church like you've never loved it before. You'll feel like you belong to it. You'll have a better relationship with its workers and love God's kingdom more, because where your investment is, there is where you will inevitably find your highest "interest."

Smith goes on to add, "If church doesn't 'interest' you, could it be because you've not made any 'investment' in it?"

Tithing is more than something we do to raise money in the church. It stands alongside worship, singing songs of praise, reading scripture, preaching, and praying in its importance to a community of faith. As an act of worship, tithing is an offering to God. As an act of community, it fulfills God's plan for the support of His Church. As an act of personal commitment, it creates a bond to the church and its leaders.

## Lessons Learned Early

Jeff and Stacey settled the issue of tithing early in their marriage. When the first paycheck as a couple came, they knew the first tenth was the Lord's.

We had just relocated, and our first income as a married couple was in our hands. It wasn't much, but it was all we had. The beginning of our shared life was taking shape. The little apartment was furnished with used furniture from family members or wedding gifts from friends. The bills began their periodic appearances in our lives: for rent, utilities, school payments, and insurances. As we held our first income in our hands and peered into the envelopes containing bills, the question was *Are we going to tithe?*

In our premarital work there had been discussions about separate or joint checking and savings accounts, about who would be responsible for paying the bills and monitoring the savings and retirement accounts, about communication and problem-solving in the marriage. But the discussion about tithing in the first weeks of our marriage was brief, about fifteen seconds. The question seemed more rhetorical than exploratory. But we have been tithing ever since that brief discussion.

As I reflect on this now, much later, I acknowledge a bit of intrigue. The decision to give away ten percent of our income could amount to hundreds of thousands of dollars over the course of a lifetime.

Jeff credits those who taught him as a child for much of his belief on tithing.

It seems Stacey and I came to digest the practices and grammar of our upbringing. Perhaps it was Sister Thomas's practice of collecting an offering during Sunday School that taught me the importance of giving to the church. Perhaps it was Pastor Hilburn's calling for the ushers to come forward to collect the congregation's tithes and offerings each week that modeled for me the practice of giving. Perhaps it was my parents' insistence on dividing my "income" between tithing, saving, and spending categories. Perhaps it was the language of prayer that taught me that God was the source of all things. Perhaps it was the grammar of the gospel causing me to realize that all that I was, as well as all that was entrusted to my care, required my faithful stewardship.

But Jeff admits there is a subtle temptation to wonder, *What if I don't tithe?* Jeff says:

I tend to ask myself that question most often when I see my neighbor making major home improvements or a friend purchasing a new car. When I experience those temptations I realize, though, that if I quit tithing I would become a different person.

Jeff credits those childhood experiences and lessons for his and Stacey's beliefs regarding tithing. He admits that it still requires a firm decision and relentless commitment. Jeff says, "It's a decision and commitment that play out each pay period, even all these years later!"

## Your Church Support Story

Tell about those who taught you about tithing.

_____

_____

_____

_____

_____

_____

_____

_____

_____

_____

_____

_____

_____

_____

_____

_____

_____

_____

_____

# ■ Think

1. Does your church beg for money? If you are the pastor, how do you approach tithes and offerings? If you are a layperson, how does your pastor approach tithes and offerings?

_____

_____

_____

_____

_____

_____

2. In most churches not everyone tithes. What ministries could your church finance if every member in the congregation were to tithe?

_____

_____

_____

_____

_____

_____

_____

3. What needs in your church and community that aren't being met now could be met if every member of the congregation tithed?

_____

_____

_____

_____

_____

_____

_____

_____

_____

_____

_____

_____

_____

_____

_____

_____

_____

_____

## ■ Discover

Read the following verses.

- "You and the Levites and the aliens among you shall rejoice in all the good things the LORD your God has given to you and your household. When you have finished setting aside a tenth of all your produce in the third year, the year of the tithe, you shall give it to the Levite, the alien, the fatherless and the widow, so that they may eat in your towns and be satisfied. Then say to the LORD your God: 'I have removed from my house the sacred portion and have given it to the Levite, the alien, the fatherless and the widow, according to all you commanded. I have not turned aside from your commands nor have I forgotten any of them'" (Deuteronomy 26:11-13).

- "He ordered the people living in Jerusalem to give the portion due the priests and Levites so they could devote themselves to the Law of the LORD. As soon as the order went out, the Israelites generously gave the firstfruits of their grain, new wine, oil and honey and all that the fields produced. They brought a great amount, a tithe of everything. The men of Israel and Judah who lived in the towns of Judah also brought a tithe of their herds and flocks and a tithe of the holy things dedicated to the LORD their God, and they piled them in heaps" (2 Chronicles 31:4-6).

- "As it is also written in the Law, we will bring the firstborn of our sons and of our cattle, of our herds and of our flocks to the house of our God, to the priests ministering there. Moreover, we will bring to the storerooms of the house of our God, to the priests, the first of our ground meal, of our grain offerings, of the fruit of all our trees and of our new wine and oil. And we will bring a tithe of our crops to the Levites, for it is the Levites who collect the tithes in all the towns where we work. A priest descended from Aaron is to accompany the Levites when they receive the tithes, and the Levites are to bring a tenth of the tithes up to the house of our God, to the storerooms of the treasury" (Nehemiah 10:36-38).

- "Will a man rob God? Yet you rob me. But you ask, 'How do we rob you?' "In tithes and offerings. You are under a curse—the whole nation of you—because you are robbing me. Bring the whole tithe into the storehouse, that there may be food in my house. Test me in this," says the Lord Almighty, "and see if I will not throw open the floodgates of heaven and pour out so much blessing that you will not have room enough for it. I will prevent pests from devouring your crops, and the vines in your fields will not cast their fruit," says the Lord Almighty" (Malachi 3:8-11).

What needs are being met in the faith community by the giving reflected in these passages?

_____

_____

_____

_____

_____

_____

_____

_____

_____

_____

# The Principle of Blessing

Bring the whole tithe into the storehouse, that there may be food in my house. Test me in this, says the LORD Almighty, "and see if I will not throw open the floodgates of heaven and pour out so much blessing that you will not have room enough for it.

—Malachi 3:10

Not once have I been witness to God's failure to supply my need when first I had given for the furtherance of His work. He has never failed in His promise, so I cannot fail in my service to Him.

—William Carey

The promise of God's blessings in Malachi 3 is just as important as Malachi's warnings against robbing God. The people had been living in a spiritual fog for many years. They needed a wakeup call, and Malachi sounded the alarm. But he went beyond the warning to stop robbing God to also remind the people of Israel of a very important principle: God blesses the tithe as well as the one who tithes.

For years the people had heard the promises of a coming Messiah. With every war and famine and hardship, they lost faith. They questioned their spiritual leaders and wondered if these promises would ever become reality. The people were discouraged; they were impatient.

Their discouragement had led them to make bad choices. They had begun to turn to sorcerers and other gods for answers. They were not following the law. They oppressed widows and orphans. They cheated laborers. They were living contrary to God's way.

They were discouraged, but God had not abandoned them. In fact, it was the other way around. It was the people of Israel who had turned away from God. They were the ones who strayed to others, looking for answers. They were the ones who failed to live as God had instructed. They were the ones who had become lax in their tithe.

Malachi's message was one of both warning and hope. He reminded the people of God's promises to their ancestors, Abraham and Jacob, and that these promises were still relevant. Hope was not lost. If the people would return to God, God would return to them (Malachi 3:7).

In order to return to God, the people would need to change their ways. A huge red flag was their failure to give their whole tithe. Their lack of faith, as exhibited by their lack of tithing, was blocking God's blessings on their lives and their nation.

In fact, God so desperately wanted them back that He offered a challenge.

"Test me in this," says the Lord Almighty, "and see if I will not throw open the floodgates of heaven and pour out so much blessing that you will not have room enough for it" *(Malachi 3:10)*.

God didn't make a habit of challenging people to test Him. But He put himself out there and dared the people to put Him to the test. He put himself and His reputation on the line.

## Jesus Makes a Promise

Jesus didn't use the word *test* or *challenge*, but He essentially said the same thing. In His Sermon on the Mount, Jesus talked about blessings as a result of giving.

> Give, and it will be given to you. A good measure, pressed down, shaken together and running over, will be poured into your lap. For with the measure you use, it will be measured to you *(Luke 6:38)*.

In the first principle of tithing—God owns it all—we looked at Jesus' challenge to avoid worry in our lives (Luke 12:22-31). Jesus reminds us in those verses that God's desire is to care for us and bless us. If we can grasp that, we can free ourselves from the worries and fears related to trusting God in our giving. God's promise, re-stated by Jesus in His own words, is still valid for us today.

## Paul and Blessings

Paul was more specific in tying the level of blessings directly to the level of giving. In 2 Corinthians 9:6 he wrote, "Remember this: Whoever sows sparingly will also reap sparingly, and whoever sows generously will also reap generously." Further, Paul said "God is able to make all grace abound to you, so that in all things at all times, having all that you need, you will abound in every good work" (2 Corinthians 9:8).

Paul touches on the Creator/Owner theme as he reminds the Corinthians that God, who is the Provider, will provide for them: "Now he who supplies seed to the sower and bread for food will also supply and increase your store of seed and will enlarge the harvest of your righteousness" (2 Corinthians 9:10).

The interesting thing about Paul's words is he indicates that God's blessings on us are intended to make us more generous, and this generosity will bring blessings and honor to God. That sounds like a wonderful cycle to me!

And giving to God is a cycle. Stan and Linda Toler picked up on this theme in their book *The Cycle of Victorious Giving:*

> In the economy of God's kingdom, we don't give in order to get something back. We simply give because we love God. We give as an expression of our appreciation for His blessings and as an expression of our loyalty to Him. And, in return, we receive sovereign benefits continually supplied in just the right amount for our spiritual good. Then, in return, we give back—we *recycle* God's blessings.[1]

A common theme flows from God's words through His prophet Malachi to Jesus' words on the mountainside and through Paul's words in his letter to the Corinthians. God desires to bless His people. He wants the best for His people. God is able and willing to provide for the needs of His people. But He is waiting for His people to express trust and faith, and a significant expression of faith is giving—more specifically, giving the tithe.

## I Am Wealthy!

Angelito wears a sticker that says, "I am wealthy because . . . I tithe!" If you compare him to world standards you might not think Angelito is wealthy. But don't try to convince *him* of that.

Angelito has faithfully tithed since he was a little boy. Growing up in the Philippines, young Angelito began tithing from income he received selling ice drops and cold water to passengers on the local train. He remembers placing ten percent from every centavo he earned in an envelope with a calendar. He would then take his tithe and place it into the church offering.

Angelito continued his commitment to tithing as he grew up, married, and had a family. As a father, Angelito taught his children the value of tithing. Now a pastor, he teaches the same lessons to his congregation.

"I can tell of numerous miracles in my life and family because of tithing," he said. "We believe in tithing. I preach it, and I live it."

Angelito's lessons were not lost on his children, who are now scattered around the world. His oldest daughter, Ammie, lives in northern California and works as a registered nurse at Stanford University Medical Center. She remembers learning about tithing as she grew up but says it really made sense to her after one of her dad's sermons.

One Sunday when I was in sixth grade my father was preaching on tithing. I remember he used the story of the little boy offering his five loaves and two fish to Jesus and how Jesus multiplied it and fed thousands. I thought about my small school allowance and money I would occasionally get for birthdays or Christmas. I realized God could use my little offering, and I began to set aside a tenth and put it in the offering plate.

Ammie continued to follow her father's example and says she is blessed because she is faithful with her tithe.

I realized growing up that I was blessed with so much. I was able to obtain a good education and then complete a nursing degree at Olivet Nazarene University. After that, I landed a good job.

Ammie credits God with blessing her life over and over, even in times of lost employment. When she had visa problems, God used people in her life and church to open doors to resolve those problems. She has found a good church home in California, where she leads worship.

"My parents still remind me to tithe," Ammie says. "I tell them, 'I still do!'"

God's blessings come in many forms. Even in the case of Angelito and his family, there were financial difficulties, illness, unemployment, and many other issues that Christians face every day. But Angelito and Ammie will quickly tell you of the many blessings God has provided.

And they know it's because they honored God with their tithe.

## Your Story of God's Blessings

How has God blessed your life? Write about a time in your life that demonstrates God's blessings.

_____

_____

_____

_____

_____

_____

_____

_____

_____

_____

_____

_____

_____

_____

_____

_____

## ■ Think

1. When you think of God's blessings, what comes to mind?

_____

_____

_____

_____

2. Does God bless us only financially when we tithe? Explain.

_____

_____

_____

_____

3. What if God asked you to put Him to the test? Would you be willing to commit to tithing for a period of time? Three months? Six months? A year?

_____

_____

_____

_____

4. If you don't currently tithe, what steps would you need to take in order to trust God and begin giving a tenth to Him?

_____

_____

_____

_____

_____

## ■ Discover

Read the following scriptures about God's blessings.

- "If you fully obey the LORD your God and carefully follow all his commands I give you today, the LORD your God will set you high above all the nations on earth. All these blessings will come upon you and accompany you if you obey the LORD your God: You will be blessed in the city and blessed in the country. The fruit of your womb will be blessed, and the crops of your land and the young of your live-stock—the calves of your herds and the lambs of your flocks. Your basket and your kneading trough will be blessed. You will be blessed when you come in and blessed when you go out. The LORD will grant that the enemies who rise up against you will be defeated before you. They will come at you from one direction but flee from you in seven. The LORD will send a blessing on your barns and on everything you put your hand to. The LORD your God will bless you in the land he is giving you. The LORD will establish you as his holy people, as he promised you on oath, if you keep the commands of the LORD your God and walk in his ways. Then all the peoples on earth will see that you are called by the name of the LORD, and they will fear you. The LORD will grant you abundant prosperity—in the fruit of your womb, the young of your livestock and the crops of your ground—in the land he swore to your forefathers to give you. The LORD will open the heavens, the storehouse of his bounty, to send rain on your land in season and to bless all the work of your hands. You will lend to many nations but will borrow from none. The LORD will make you the head, not the tail. If you pay attention to the commands of the LORD your God that I give you this day and carefully follow them, you will always be at the top, never at the bottom. Do not turn aside from any of the commands I give you today, to the right or to the left, following other gods and serving them" (Deuteronomy 28:1-14).

- "Vindicate me, O LORD, for I have led a blameless life; I have trusted in the LORD without wavering. Test me, O LORD, and try me, examine my heart and my mind; for your love is ever before me, and I walk continually in your truth. I do not sit with deceitful men, nor do I consort with hypocrites; I abhor the assembly of evildoers and refuse to sit with the wicked. I wash my hands in innocence, and go about your altar, O LORD, proclaiming aloud your praise and telling of all your wonderful deeds. I love the house where you live, O LORD, the place where your glory dwells. Do not take away my soul along with sinners, my life with bloodthirsty men, in whose hands are wicked schemes, whose right hands are full of bribes. But I lead a blameless life; redeem me and be merciful to me. My feet stand on level ground; in

the great assembly I will praise the LORD"
(Psalm 26).

- "Blessed is he who has regard for the
  weak; the LORD delivers him in times of
  trouble. The LORD will protect him and pre-
  serve his life; he will bless him in the land
  and not surrender him to the desire of his
  foes. The LORD will sustain him on his sick-
  bed and restore him from his bed of illness" (Psalm 41:1-3).

What can these verses teach you about trusting God?

_____

_____

_____

_____

_____

_____

_____

# Notes

## Chapter 2

1. Brother Andrew, John Sherrill, and Elizabeth Sherrill, *The Narrow Road* (Grand Rapids: Fleming H. Revell, 2001), 102-103.

## Chapter 4

1. Collin Hansen, "The Ancient Rise and Recent Fall of Tithing," christianhistory.net, August 8, 2008, <http://www.christianitytoday.com/ch/news/2003/jun6.html>.

2. Kauffman, Milo, *Stewards of God* (Scottsdale, Pa.: Herald Press, 1975), 188.

3. Henry Lansdell, *The Tithe in Scripture* (Grand Rapids: Baker Book House, 1963), 125.

4. Kauffman, *Stewards of God*, 189.

## Chapter 5

1. Stan and Linda Toler, *The Cycle of Victorious Giving* (Kansas City: Beacon Hill Press of Kansas City, 2004), 14.

# Tithing: A Bibliography

Several good resources on the subject of tithing are available. Some are hard to find. Here is a list of resources that helped shape the discussion in this book.

Johnson, Douglas W. *The Tithe: Challenge or Legalism?* Nashville: Abingdon Press, 1984.

Kendall, R. T. *Tithing: Discover the Freedom of Biblical Giving.* Grand Rapids: Zondervan Publishing House, 1982.

Lane, Charles R. *Ask, Thank, Tell: Improving Stewardship Ministry in Your Congregation.* Minneapolis: Augsburg Fortress, 2006.

Lansdell, Henry. *The Sacred Tenth V2: Or Studies in Tithe-Giving, Ancient and Modern.* London: Society for Promoting Christian Knowledge, 1906.

_____. *The Tithe in Scripture.* Grand Rapids: Baker Book House, 1963.

# What are you doing this Lenten season?

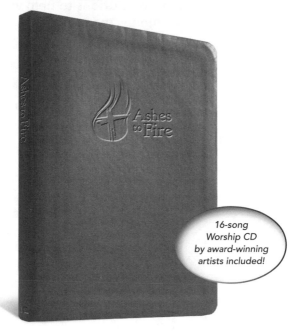

16-song Worship CD by award-winning artists included!

This 14-week devotional book includes daily scripture readings from the Old Testament and New Testament, prayers, and each Sunday, a small sermon with journaling space. *Ashes to Fire Devotional* is specifically designed to be used, either individually or for small groups, from Ash Wednesday to Pentecost.

(also available within *Ashes to Fire Church Planning Kit*)

---

**Ashes to Fire Devotional**
Edited by Merritt J. Nielson
ISBN 978-0-8341-2592-6
Synthetic Leather   $19.99

# Manage your net worth
# with new perspective.

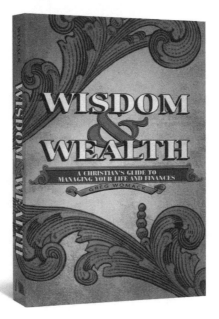

This beneficial resource will show you how to successfully
manage your finances and learn to put your money where your
faith is. Greg Womack, a certified financial planner, uses the
time-tested wisdom of King Solomon to help you make wise
financial choices, manage your money properly, and use what
you have to bless and serve others.

**WISDOM AND WEALTH**
*A Christian's Guide to Managing Your Life
and Finances*
Greg Womack
978-0-8341-2321-2

BEACON HILL PRESS
OF KANSAS CITY

www.beaconhillbooks.com